DICTIONARY SKILLS

by Sylvia J. Foust

Teacher Created Materials, Inc.
P.O. Box 1040
Huntington Beach, CA 92647
©1986 Teacher Created Materials, Inc.
Made in U.S.A.

ISBN 1-55734-339-X

The classroom teacher may reproduce copies of materials in this book for classroom use only. The reproduction of any part for an entire school or school system is strictly prohibited. No part of this publication may be transmitted, stored, or recorded in any form without written permission from the publisher.

TABLE OF CONTENTS
Dictionary Skills

TABLE OF CONTENTS

© *Teacher Created Materials, Inc. 1986*

WHAT CAN YOU LEARN FROM A DICTIONARY?

Look up these words in a dictionary and read the definitions. Use the words to complete the puzzle.

THE LIST IS ENDLESS!

pronunciation   acronym   capital

abbreviations   synonyms   illustrations

etymology   antonyms

syllables   meanings

ACROSS

1. Dictionaries help you understand definitions by showing _____ for some words.

3. An _____ is made from the first letters of a name or a group of words and is pro-nounced as one word. You can find the definition in a dictionary.

4. A dictionary gives the _____ or definitions of words.

6. Words that mean the same, or _____, are often given.

8. You can learn how to say a word, or its _____.

DOWN

2. _____ , or shortened forms of words, are listed.

5. You can find out where a word came from, or its _____ .

7. You can learn which words begin with _____ letters.

9. A dictionary will help you find _____, or opposites, of words.

10. From the phonetic spellings you can find out how many _____ a word has.

WHO IS A PAIN IN THE NECK ANY TIME OF THE YEAR?

To find out, cut along the heavy lines. Rearrange the pieces in alphabetical order, reading in a clockwise direction. Paste on another sheet of paper.

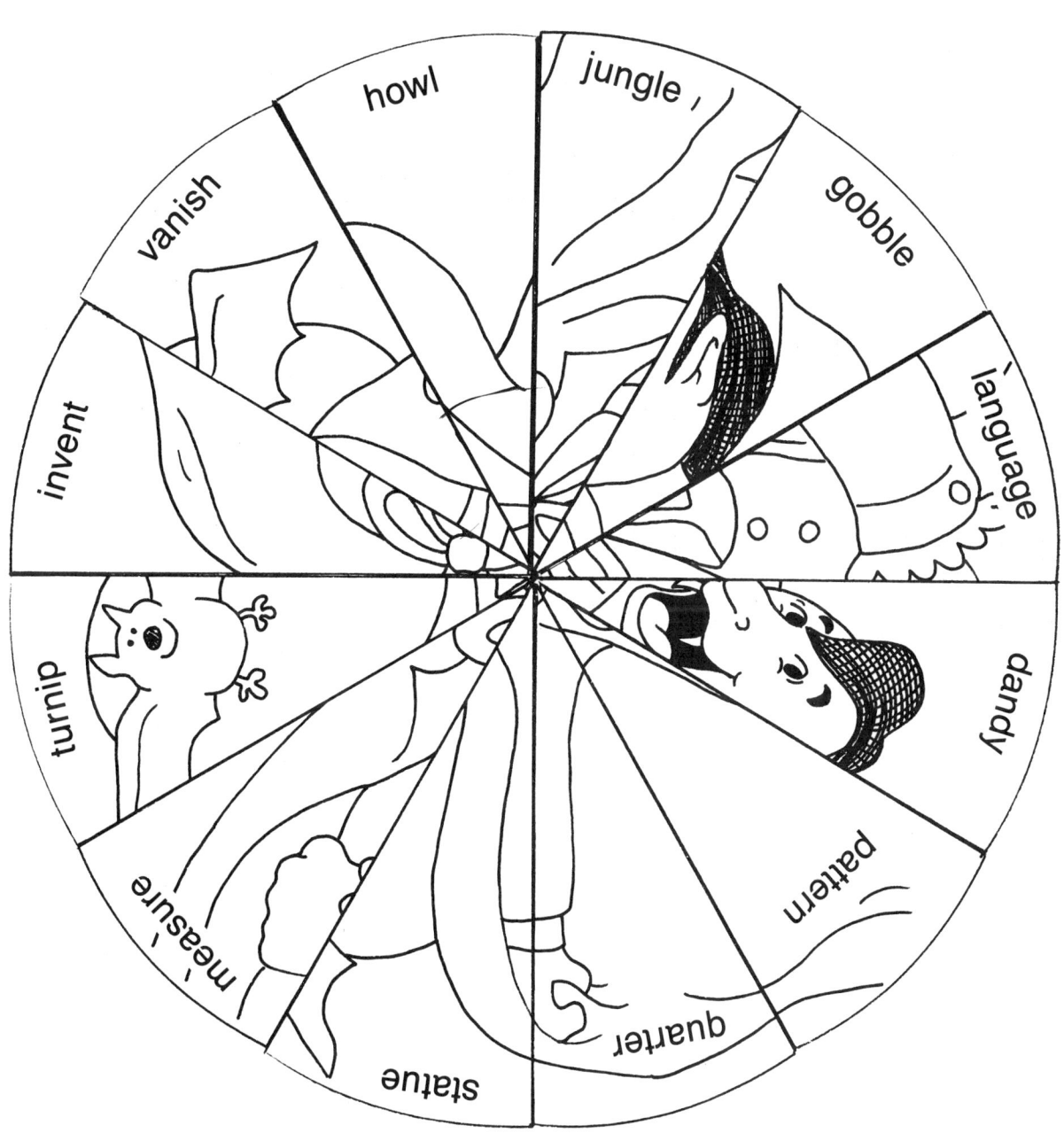

 © Teacher Created Materials, Inc. 1986

MR. FRED'S MIXED-UP FILES

Think of the dictionary as having four sections like the ones on the file cabinet. Some sections have more letters than others. This is because some letters begin more words. Write each word in the correct section.

money
huge
vacant
aunt
jam
stray
ready
desert
open
exit
wood
canvas
pet
garage
zebra
begin
pair
landing
creek
underneath

ABCD
_____
_____
_____
_____

EFGHIJKL
_____
_____
_____
_____

MNOPQR
_____
_____
_____
_____

STUVWXYZ
_____
_____
_____
_____

© Teacher Created Materials, Inc. 1986

CASE OF THE MISSING BIRD

Farmer Sal wants to buy a pet, but the bird he wants is nowhere to be found! Number the bird names in alphabetical order. Write the letters in the matching numbered blanks below to find the missing bird.

FLAMINGO
T

CROW
H

PIGEON
K

EAGLE
H

SEAGULL
I

STARLING
I

EGRET
B

FINCH
E

PEACOCK
E

OSTRICH
C

KINGFISHER
N

CANARY
G

OSPREY
C

$\overline{6}$ $\overline{2}$ $\overline{10}$ $\quad$ $\overline{4}$ $\overline{13}$ $\overline{1}$

$\overline{8}$ $\overline{3}$ $\overline{12}$ $\overline{9}$ $\overline{11}$ $\overline{5}$ $\overline{7}$!

7

© Teacher Created Materials, Inc. 1986

PAPER BOY

Look at each pair of words. Write a word that comes between the two words alphabetically. Check with a dictionary if you need help.

force
_____
forgive

rare
_____
rat

second
_____
sediment

kitchen
_____
knot

base
_____
battle

monkey
_____
moose

lamb
_____
lash

helmet
_____
herb

cape
_____
cartoon

mayor
_____
meat

© Teacher Created Materials, Inc. 1986

HOW DOES RALPH GET READY FOR A TEST?

The pair of words at the top of a dictionary page are **guide words.** They are the first and last words defined on that page. The other words are listed in alphabetical order between them.

Decide if the words in each set would be found on a page with the bold face guide words. Circle the letter in the correct column. Write the letters in the blanks below.

decide-declare

	YES	NO
1. decent	J	I
2. deck	P	M
3. decimal	B	A
4. decline	H	L

grain-grass

	YES	NO
5. grand	O	E
6. graft	K	I
7. gram	T	R
8. graze	N	U

inch-Indian

	YES	NO
9. indict	L	G
10. indebt	H	A
11. India	L	C
12. incense	X	N

oat-obstruct

	YES	NO
13. obscure	A	K
14. obey	N	G
15. obtain	R	N
16. oak	P	Y

__ __   __ __ __ __ __ __   __ __   __ __ __   __ __ __ __ __!
3 16   3 5 12 1 14 9   8 2   13 11 4   15 6 9 10 7

© Teacher Created Materials, Inc. 1986

WHY DO SPIDERS SPIN WEBS?

Look at each pair of imaginary guide words. Circle the letter of the word that **would not** be found on the same page as those guide words.

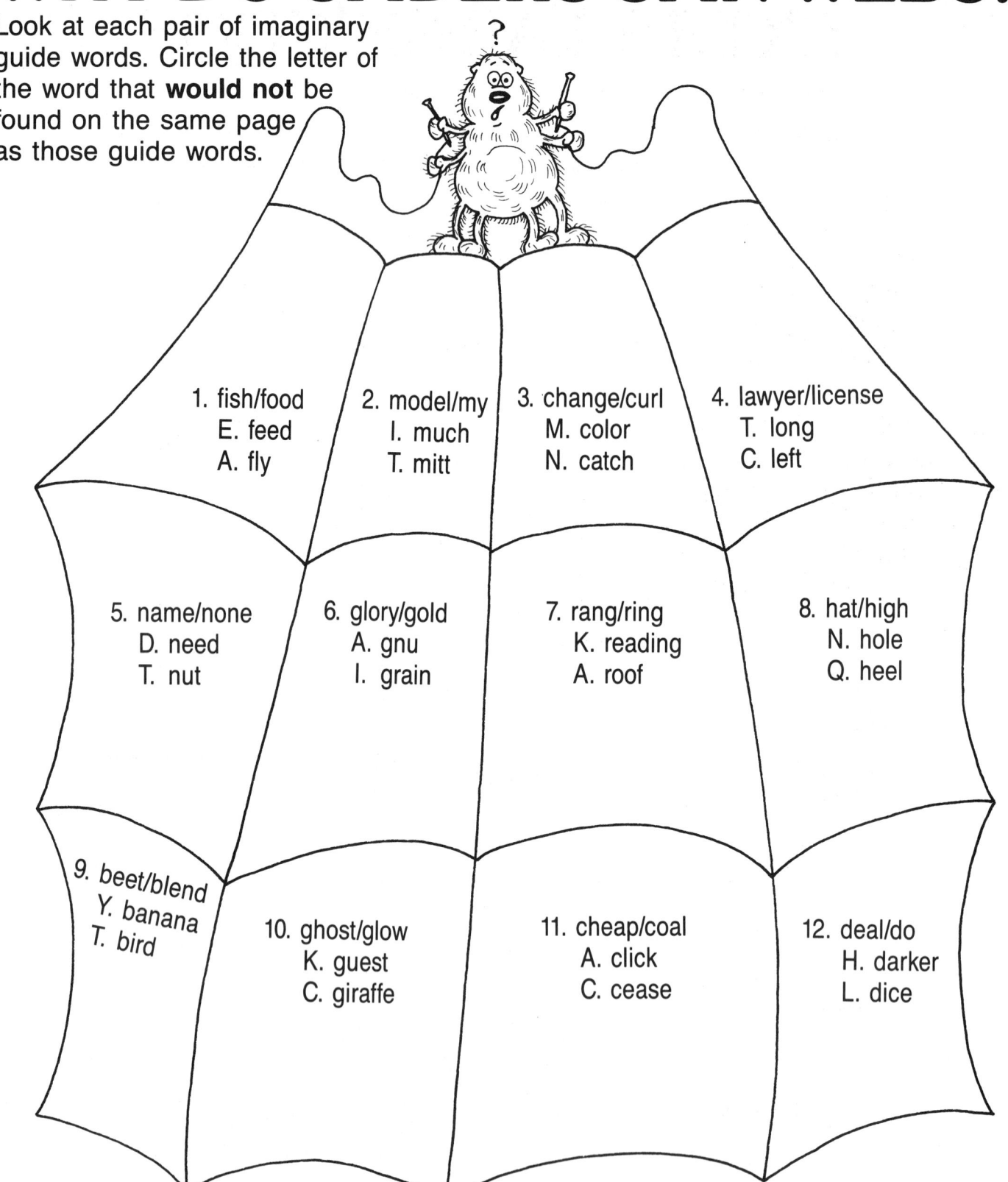

1. fish/food
   E. feed
   A. fly

2. model/my
   I. much
   T. mitt

3. change/curl
   M. color
   N. catch

4. lawyer/license
   T. long
   C. left

5. name/none
   D. need
   T. nut

6. glory/gold
   A. gnu
   I. grain

7. rang/ring
   K. reading
   A. roof

8. hat/high
   N. hole
   Q. heel

9. beet/blend
   Y. banana
   T. bird

10. ghost/glow
    K. guest
    C. giraffe

11. cheap/coal
    A. click
    C. cease

12. deal/do
    H. darker
    L. dice

Now write the circled letters in the matching numbered blanks.

BECAUSE __ __ __ __   __ __ __ __   __ __ __ __ !
         4 12 1 9   11 7 3 5   10 8 6 2

© Teacher Created Materials, Inc. 1986

EXTRA-LARGE EGGS

color   check   cracker   crab
canopy   coy   candle   cheetah
comic   combine   colony   camel
    calves   chef
    cheat   cowboy

Which of these imaginary guide-word pairs would each word belong under? Write the words on the correct eggs.

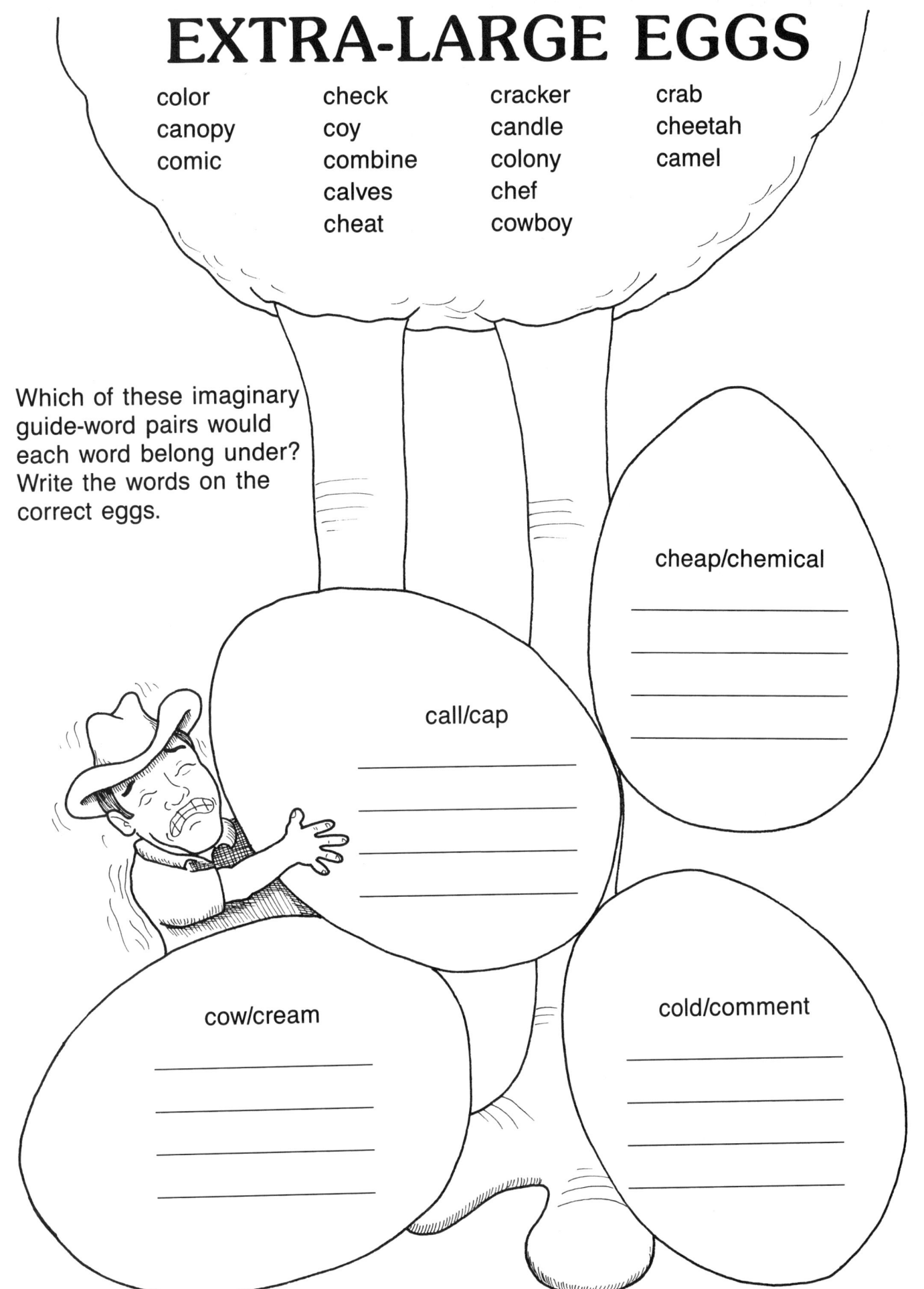

cheap/chemical

call/cap

cow/cream

cold/comment

11   © Teacher Created Materials, Inc. 1986

DOWN LONGHORN LANE

Head 'em up and move 'em out, pardner! Find each word in your dictionary. Write the guide words from that page on each horn.

spunk   spurs   spy

Sample

herd

mustang

buckboard

sagebrush

coyote

bronco

longhorn

canteen

prairie

lariat

Answers will vary depending on dictionary used.

© Teacher Created Materials, Inc. 1986

12

CATCH THOSE CRITTERS!

It hasn't been a very good day for zookeeper Carl! All of the animals have escaped! Help catch those critters! Locate each word in a dictionary and write the guide words from that page.

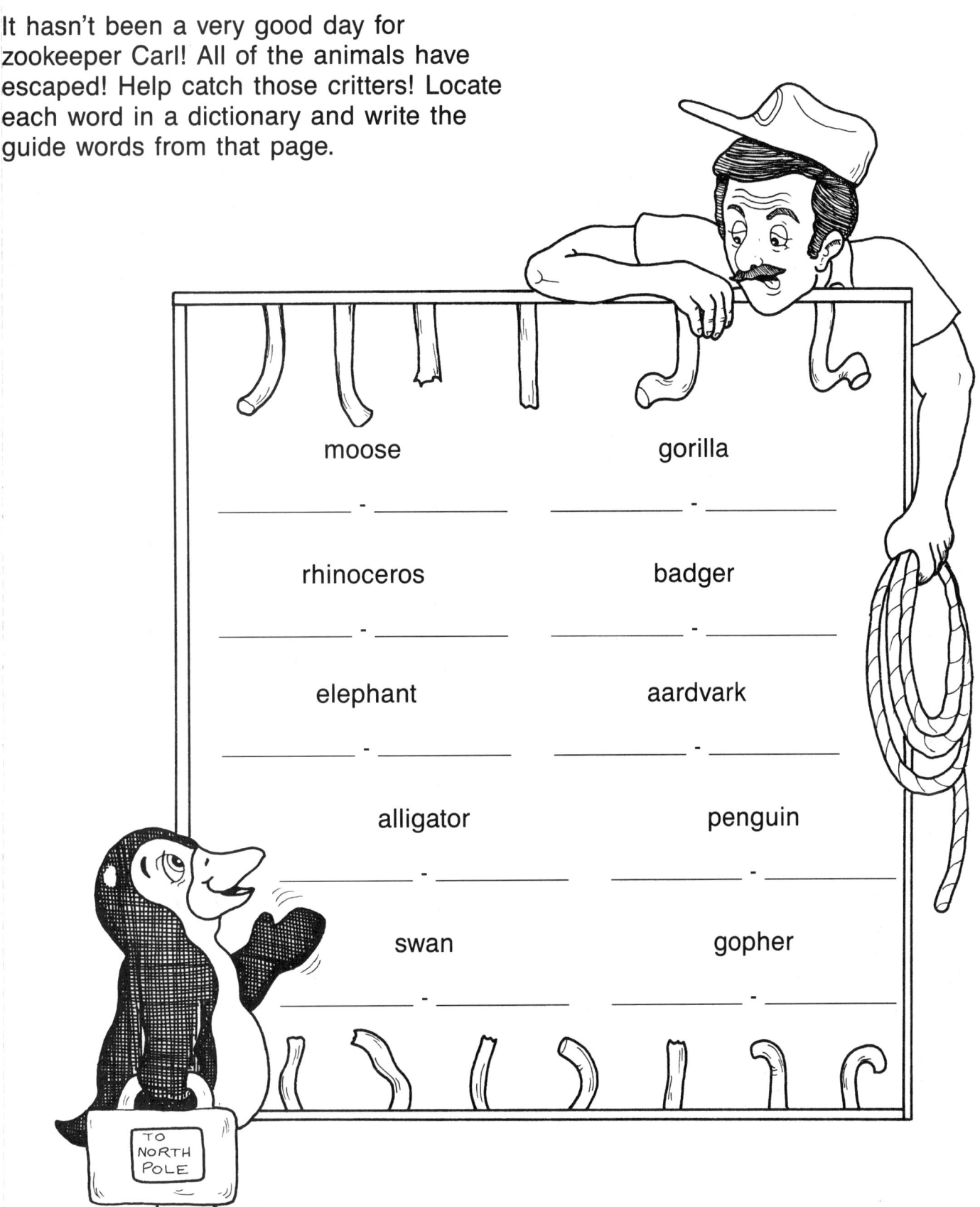

moose

_____ - _____

gorilla

_____ - _____

rhinoceros

_____ - _____

badger

_____ - _____

elephant

_____ - _____

aardvark

_____ - _____

alligator

_____ - _____

penguin

_____ - _____

swan

_____ - _____

gopher

_____ - _____

Now choose one animal. On the back describe how you would keep it as a pet!

© Teacher Created Materials, Inc. 1986

AN ABSENT-MINDED PROFESSOR

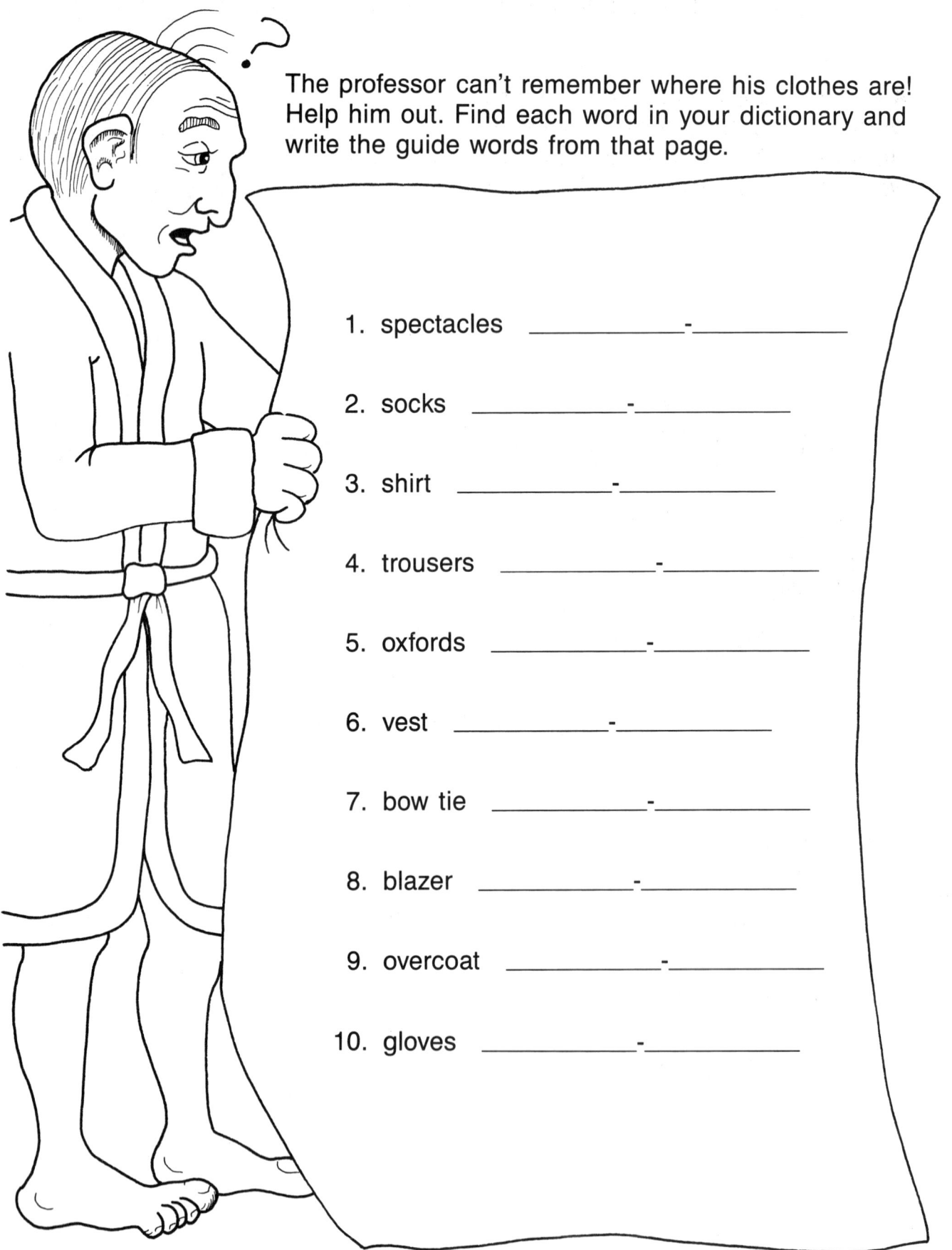

The professor can't remember where his clothes are!
Help him out. Find each word in your dictionary and
write the guide words from that page.

1. spectacles _____-_____

2. socks _____-_____

3. shirt _____-_____

4. trousers _____-_____

5. oxfords _____-_____

6. vest _____-_____

7. bow tie _____-_____

8. blazer _____-_____

9. overcoat _____-_____

10. gloves _____-_____

Now draw the professor on the back of this sheet. He should be dressed and ready
for class!

© Teacher Created Materials, Inc. 1986   14

FANCY FENCE

A compound entry contains two or more words. When used together, the words have a special meaning and are listed together in a dictionary. However, not all words used together are compound entries. Look for these word pairs in a dictionary. Draw a shape around the compound entries.

boiling point

river bed

brown bear

canary yellow

rubber band

station wagon

pocket book

flying saucer

hair spray

candle power

shower cap

potato chip

 © Teacher Created Materials, Inc. 1986

WHERE CAN YOU ALWAYS FIND TIME?

The words on the left are written phonetically. Write the letters of the words on the right in the matching blanks. Then read down the letters.

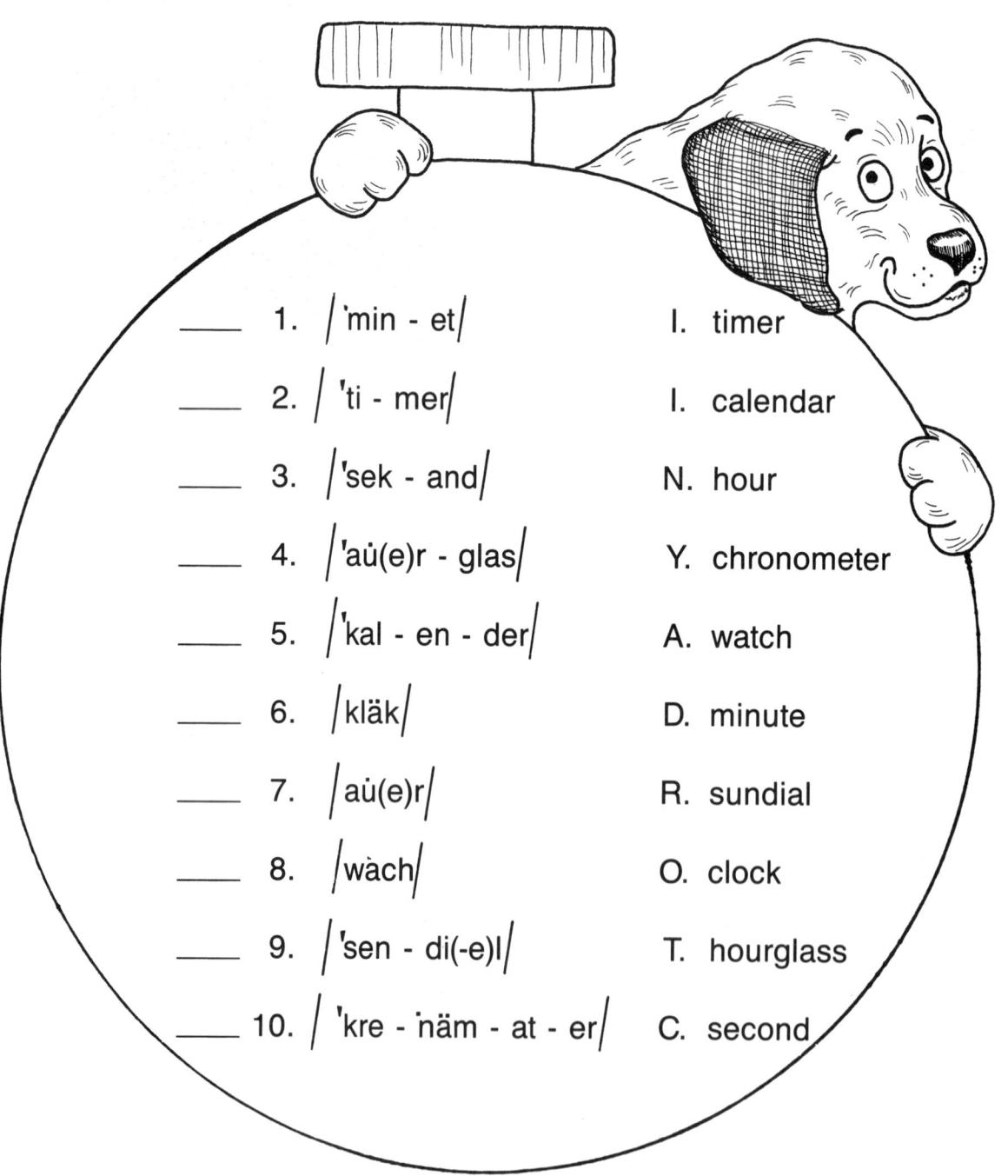

_____ 1. /ˈmin - et/   I. timer

_____ 2. /ˈti - mer/   I. calendar

_____ 3. /ˈsek - and/   N. hour

_____ 4. /ˈau̇(e)r - glas/   Y. chronometer

_____ 5. /ˈkal - en - der/   A. watch

_____ 6. /kläk/   D. minute

_____ 7. /au̇(e)r/   R. sundial

_____ 8. /wäch/   O. clock

_____ 9. /ˈsen - di(-e)l/   T. hourglass

_____ 10. /ˈkre - ˌnäm - at - er/   C. second

You can always find time in a _____!

© Teacher Created Materials, Inc. 1986

MESSAGE IN A BOTTLE

These words are written phonetically, or the way they are spoken. Use the pronunciation key in your dictionary to help you read them. Rewrite each word correctly under its phonetic spelling.

Hělp,

_____

Ī'm 'stran - dəd ȯn an 'ī - land.

_____

Plēz send ā bōt 'kwik - lē. Ī

_____

dōnt wänt tü lēv. Ī jəst nēd

_____

a 'tel - ə - vizh - ən and ā 'ver - ē

_____

lȯn i -'lek - tri - kəl kȯ(ə)rd.

_____

Robin

Now write a response to the person who sent this note! Use the back of this sheet.

 © Teacher Created Materials, Inc. 1986

WHAT IS THE BEST WAY TO TALK TO A MARTIAN?

Circle only the two-syllable words. Draw a line through the maze to connect those words. Write the letters found under the circled words in order below.

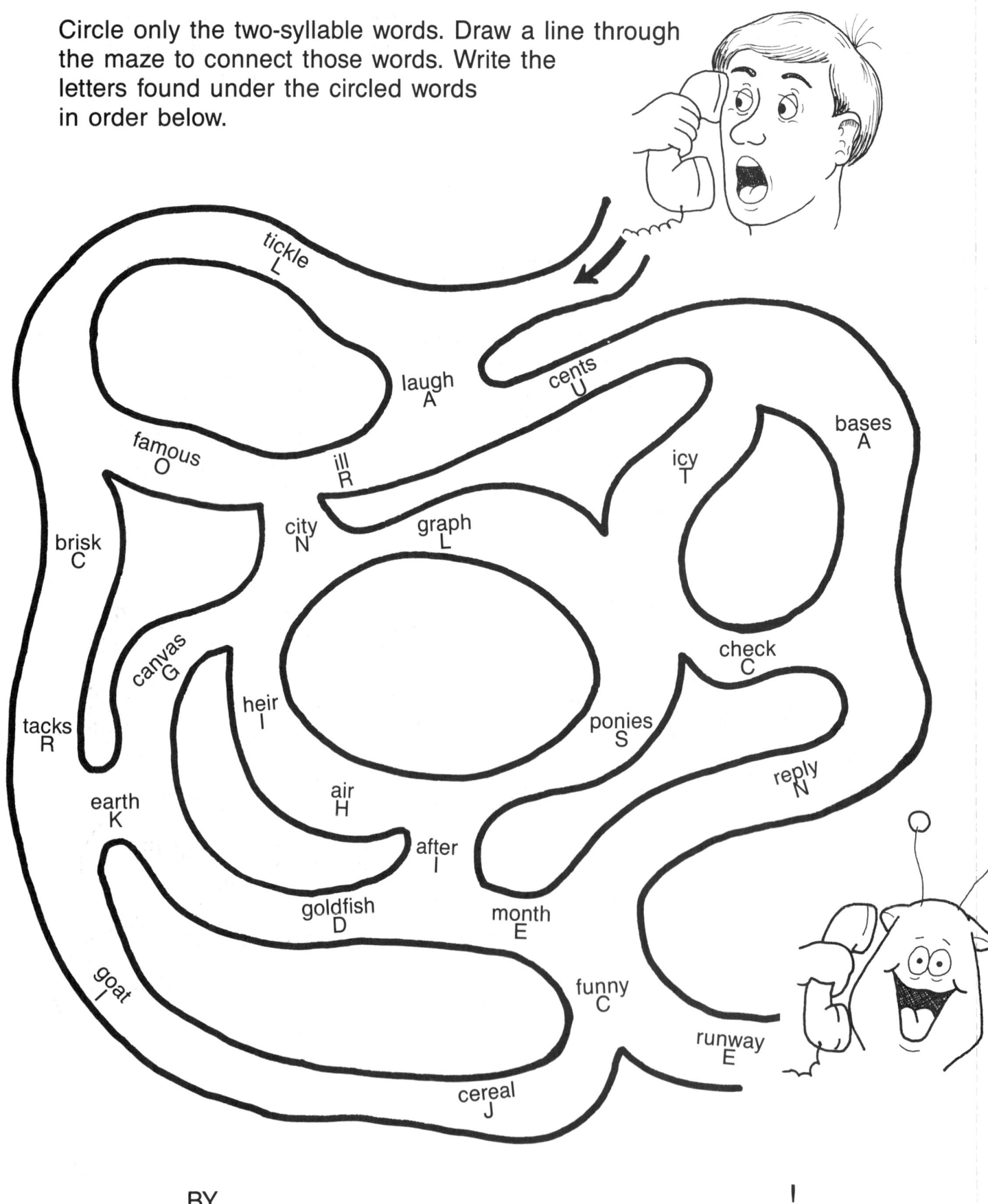

tickle
L

laugh
A

cents
U

bases
A

famous
O

ill
R

icy
T

brisk
C

city
N

graph
L

canvas
G

check
C

heir
I

ponies
S

tacks
R

reply
N

earth
K

air
H

after
I

goldfish
D

month
E

goat
I

funny
C

runway
E

cereal
J

BY _ _ _ _ _   _ _ _ _ _ _ !

PEACOCK ROCK

Read each word and count the syllables. Check a dictionary if you need help.

Color: one-syllable words - yellow
two-syllable words - orange
three-syllable words - green
four-syllable words - purple

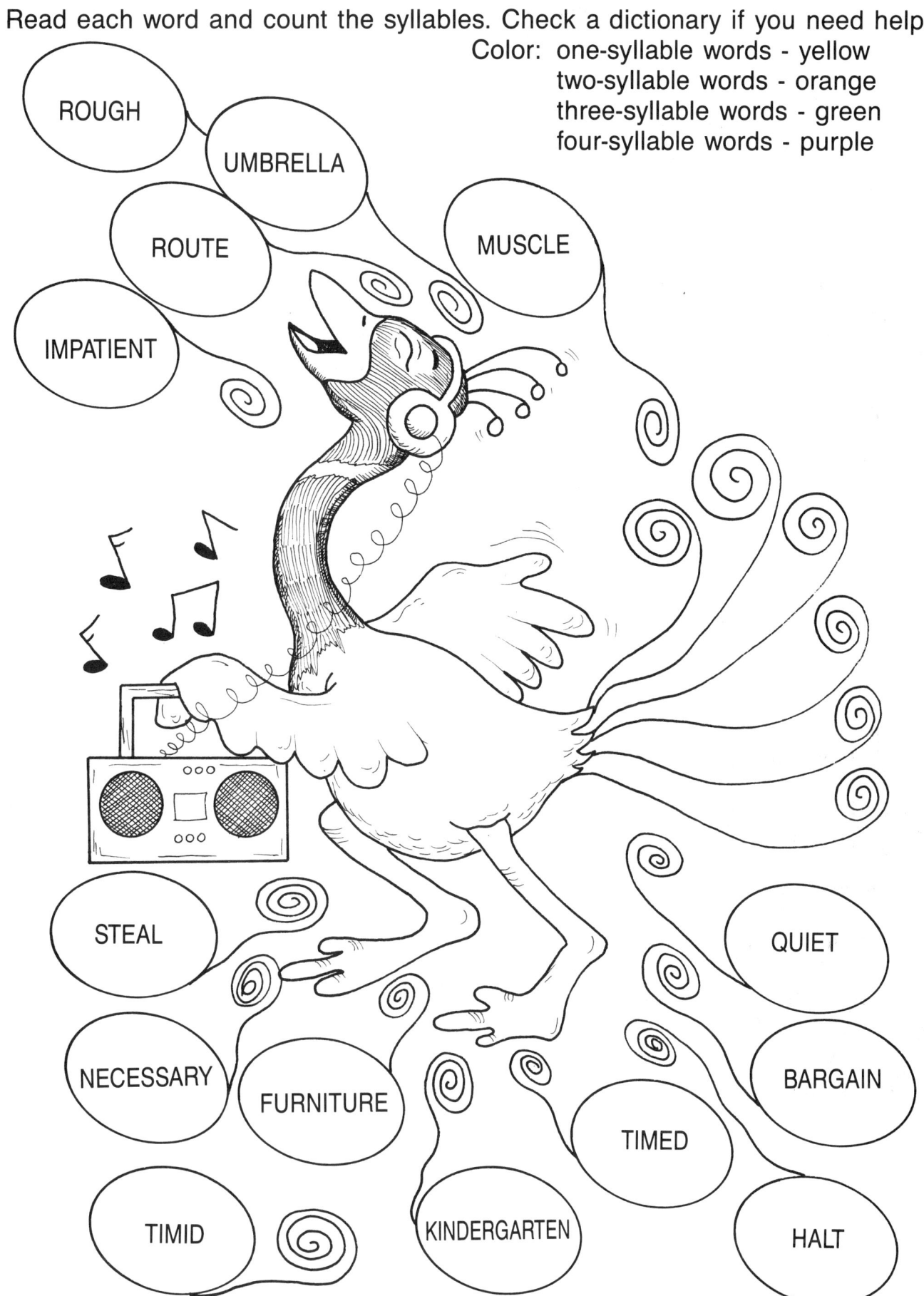

 © Teacher Created Materials, Inc. 1986

SHOPPING SPREE

Say each word to yourself. Which syllables are stressed? Mark each accented syllable as shown. Be careful — some words have secondary accents. Check yourself with a dictionary.

SAMPLE: straw′ ber″ ry

Groceries

to ma to   (soup)

pump kins   (2 large)

ba nan a   (1)

pep pers

cab bage   (2 lbs.)

tur nips

blue ber ry   (jam)

sau sage   (1 lb.)

lem on ade   (1 qt.)

po ta toes   (a bag)

wa ter mel on

oat meal   (a box)

Now imagine you could go through the grocery store and fill up one cart — FREE! On the back, describe the things you would put in your cart.

© Teacher Created Materials, Inc. 1986

KEEP COOL!

When a word won't fit on a line, you must divide it between the syllables.

Rewrite each word, putting one syllable on a line. Remember to use a hyphen between each syllable.

Use a dictionary if you need help.

1. eyelash _____ _____

2. slender _____ _____

3. peaceful _____ _____

4. chimpanzee_____ _____ _____

5. willow _____ _____

6. bathtub _____ _____

7. saddle _____ _____

8. yesterday _____ _____ _____

9. chicken _____ _____

10. opossum _____ _____ _____

11. umbrella _____ _____ _____

12. balloons _____ _____

Now think of five ways to keep a polar bear cool! Write them on the back.

© Teacher Created Materials, Inc. 1986

WHAT CAN YOU SEE ONCE IN A MINUTE, ONCE IN A MONTH, BUT NEVER IN A HUNDRED YEARS?

Each of these words has a consonant sound between two vowel sounds. Follow these rules and color each section to answer the riddle.

Color Yellow:
Divide a word before the consonant when the first vowel sound is long.
sha / dy

Color Blue:
Divide a word after the consonant when the first vowel sound is short.
pun / ish

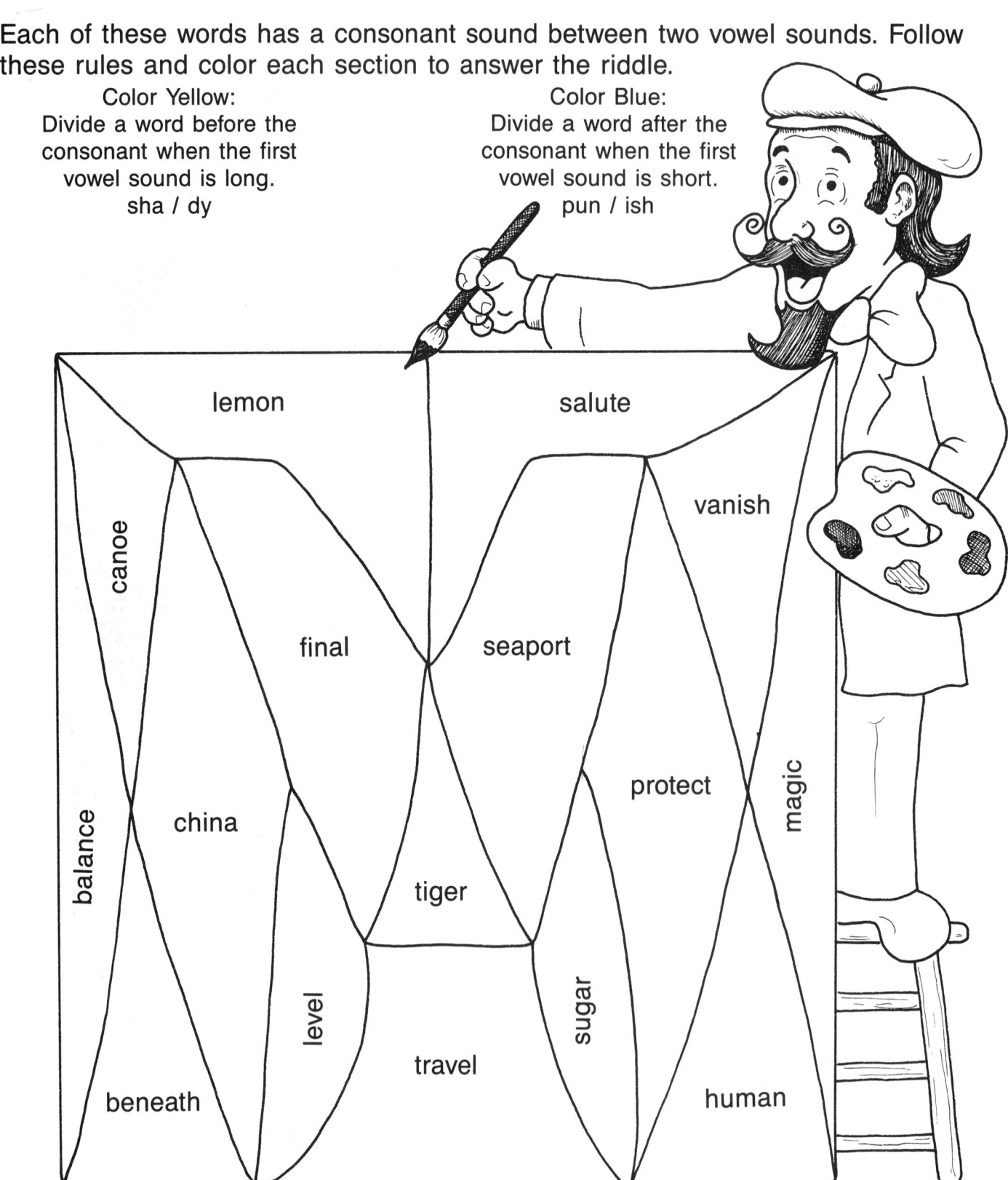

lemon

salute

canoe

vanish

balance

final

seaport

china

protect

magic

tiger

level

sugar

beneath

travel

human

© Teacher Created Materials, Inc. 1986

GOLD RUSH!

The gold rush in on! Stake your claim on this nine-hundred pound nugget! For each word, write the suffix and the definition of the word. Use a dictionary if you need help. Remember: a suffix is a letter or letters added to the end of a root word.

	Suffix	Definition
1. thankful	ful	
2. amazement		
3. yearly		
4. electrical		
5. protective		
6. artist		
7. neatness		
8. volcanic		
9. silently		
10. thickness		

© Teacher Created Materials, Inc. 1986

WHAT ALWAYS WORKS BETTER WHEN IT IS USED UP?

Choose a word from below to complete each sentence. Use a dictionary if you need help. Then cut and paste the strips in order vertically on your own paper.

1. If you make directions more simple, you _____ them.

2. A person who bakes is a _____.

3. If a painting is full of beauty, it is _____.

4. If the tag on your jacket says to clean it in water, it is _____.

5. When a person doesn't have a penny, he is _____.

6. The place where bread is baked is the _____.

7. When a person has a lot of skill, he is _____.

8. A person who teaches is a _____.

9. The state of being a child is called _____.

10. A table made from wood is a _____ table.

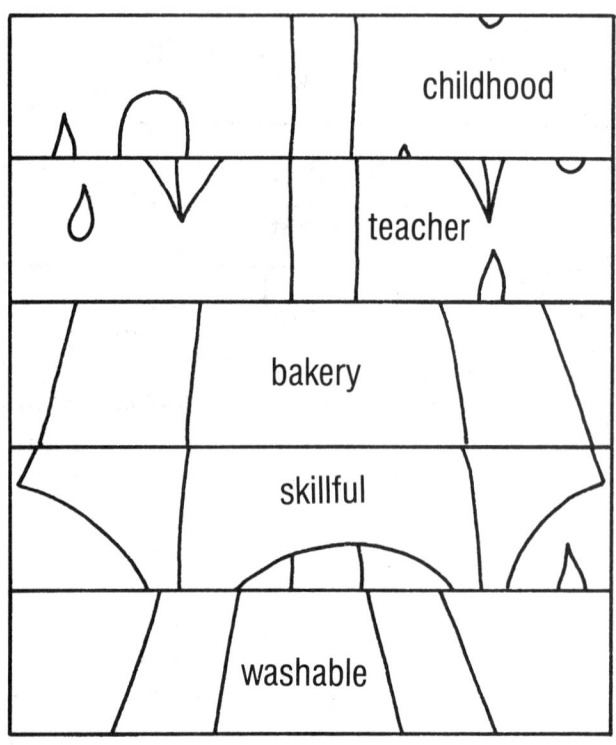

childhood

teacher

bakery

skillful

washable

wooden

beautiful

simplify

baker

penniless

© Teacher Created Materials, Inc. 1986

IF CHEESE COMES ON TOP OF A CHEESEBURGER, WHAT COMES AFTER THE CHEESE?

Choose a word from below to complete each sentence. Use a dictionary if you need help. Then cut and paste the strips in order vertically on your own paper.

1. A question that is confusing may be _____ .

2. If you pay for an item before you pick it up, you _____.

3. When you soak your dirty socks before washing them, you _____ them.

4. When you don't understand the directions on a test, you _____.

5. If the teacher asks you to write a report again, you _____ it.

6. A magazine that comes every two months is _____.

7. When you pay more than you owe, you _____.

8. Someone who is against all wars is _____.

9. The middle of the night is called _____.

10. When you arrange your papers a second time, you _____ them.

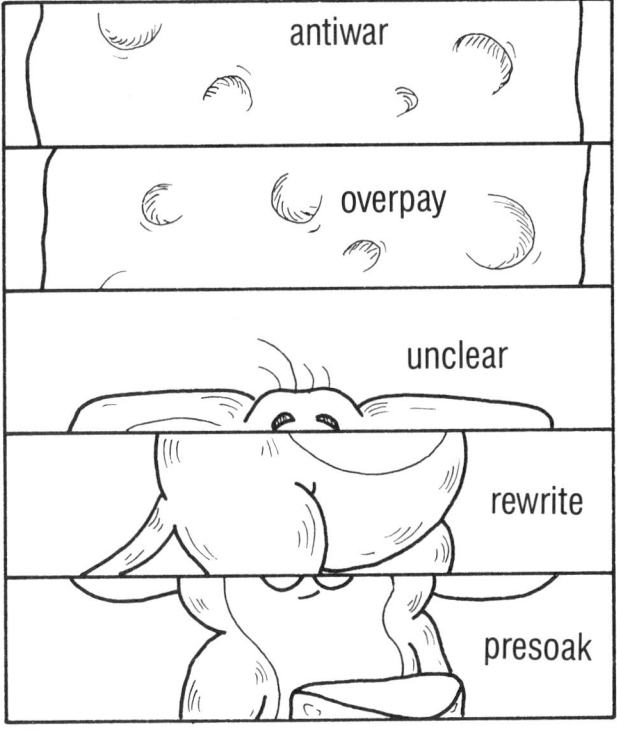

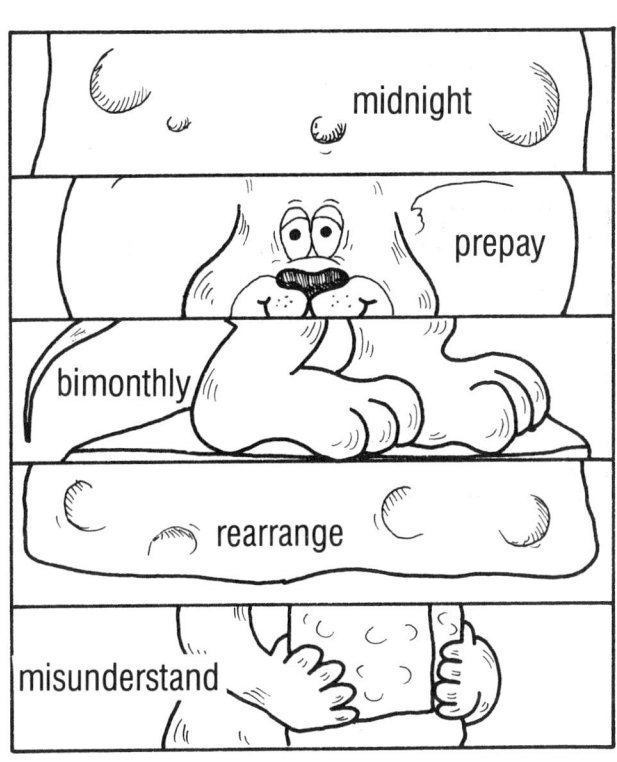

antiwar

overpay

unclear

rewrite

presoak

midnight

prepay

bimonthly

rearrange

misunderstand

© Teacher Created Materials, Inc. 1986

TEST YOUR STRENGTH!

How many new words can you make?

MAGNIFICENT!

Prefixes	Root Words
dis-	cycle
(apart from, not)	
	clear
auto- (self)	
	pack
un- (not)	
	weekly
bi- (two)	
	glue
re- (again)	
	bus
	tie
	obey
	harp
	locate
	biography

15. _____

14. _____

13. _____

12. _____

11. _____

10. _____

9. _____

8. _____

7. _____

6. _____

5. _____

4. _____

3. _____

2. _____

1. _____

Combine these prefixes and root words. Write each new word on a line, starting at the arrow. Then check yourself with a dictionary. If you get 15 correct words, you're MAGNIFICENT!

© Teacher Created Materials, Inc. 1986

WATCH THE BIRDIE!

Mark through the prefix and suffix in each word. Write the root words below.

1. reappearance
2. mistrustful
3. impersonal
4. discouragement
5. unthinkable
6. prepayment
7. incorrectly
8. prearrangement
9. reaction
10. reattachment
11. enjoyable

1. __appear_____

2. _____

3. _____

4. _____

5. _____

6. _____

7. _____

8. _____

9. _____

10. _____

11. _____

© Teacher Created Materials, Inc. 1986

HOW CAN YOU TELL WHEN THERE IS AN ELEPHANT IN YOUR REFRIGERATOR?

The abbreviation following a dictionary entry tells what part of speech the word is. These are the abbreviations used most often.

a. or adj. - adjective   prep. - preposition

adv. - adverb   v. - verb

n. - noun

Locate each word in your dictionary. Circle the letter in the correct part of speech column.

	n.	adj.	v.	adv.	prep.
1. quiche	D	A	E	S	M
2. often	Q	L	N	T	O
3. awesome	B	H	C	N	D
4. peruse	I	D	N	E	O
5. with	J	C	F	G	H
6. cleverly	P	K	H	R	E
7. quaff	L	A	T	A	B
8. thyme	W	M	B	C	E
9. dormant	A	O	D	B	H
10. warily	F	C	G	U	F
11. for	H	A	I	G	O
12. clovelet	S	I	D	B	G
13. by	C	H	E	F	E
14. parch	I	E	T	G	H
15. genteel	I	O	F	I	M

Now write the circled letters in the matching numbered blanks.

$\overline{}\ \overline{}\ \overline{}$ $\overline{}\ \overline{}\ \overline{}\ \overline{}$ $\overline{}\ \overline{}\ \overline{}\ \overline{}$ $\overline{}\ \overline{}\ \overline{}\ \overline{}$!
14 5 13   1 15 9 6   8 11 4 7   12 3 10 2

© Teacher Created Materials, Inc. 1986

UNDER THE BIG TOP

Locate these words in your dictionary. After each, write the part of speech: noun, verb, adjective, adverb. Then use the word correctly in a sentence about the circus. Use your imagination and think of everything you might see under the "big top"!

1. juggled _____ _____

_____

2. clownish _____ _____

_____

3. vendor _____ _____

_____

4. paraded _____ _____

_____

5. fearlessly _____ _____

_____

6. colorful _____ _____

_____

7. trapeze _____ _____

_____

8. gaily _____ _____

_____

9. elephantine _____ _____

_____

10. ringmaster _____ _____

_____

Now choose one of your sentences and draw a picture for it on the back.

© Teacher Created Materials, Inc. 1986

BAKER'S DOZEN

Sometimes when you check a spelling in a dictionary, you have to look in more than one place. The beginning sounds of some words are the same although they're spelled differently. If you didn't know how to spell joy, you might look under g first. Use a dictionary and complete each word correctly. Then color.

r - yellow   g - orange

rh - green   j - blue

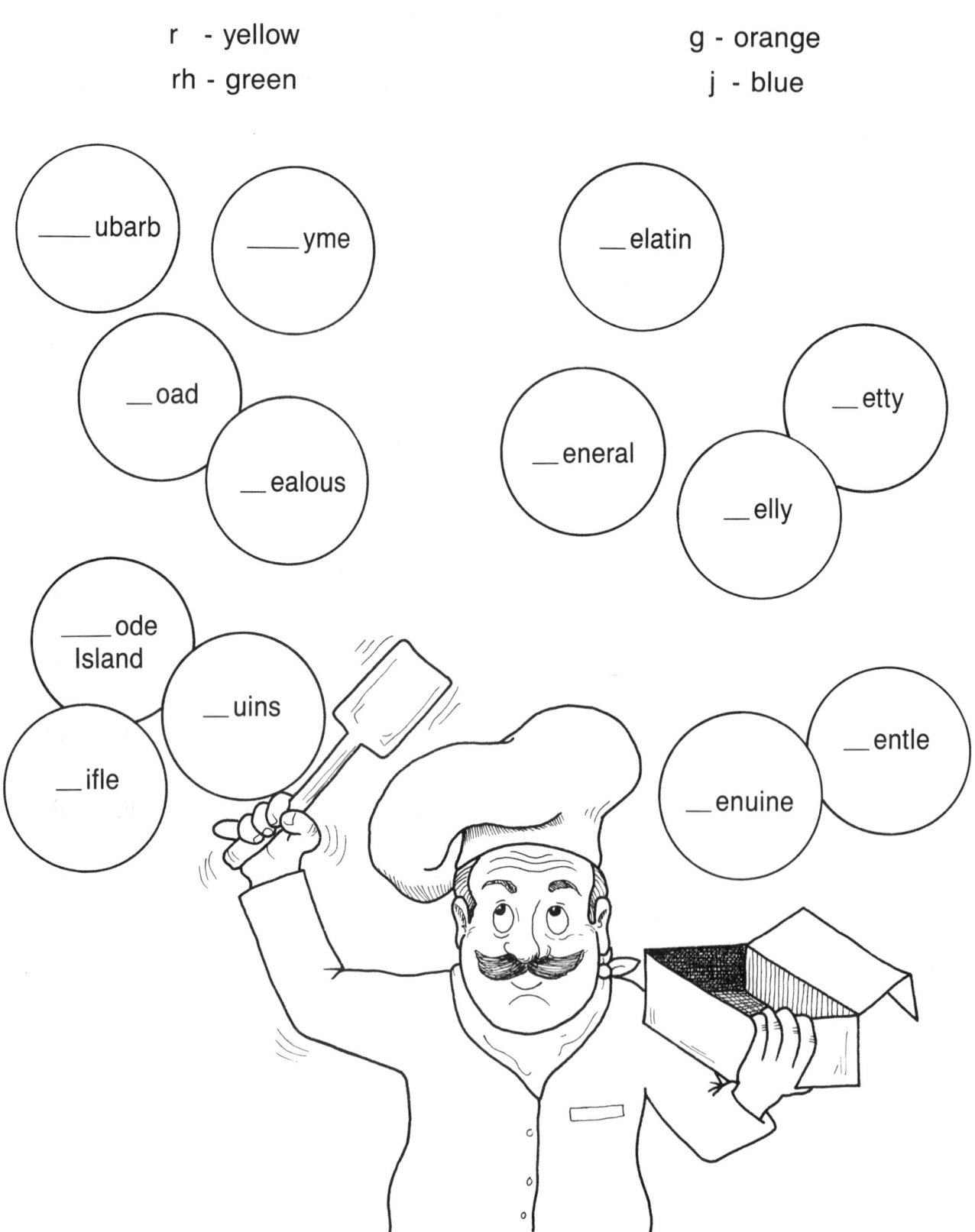

___ubarb

___yme

_elatin

_oad

_ealous

_eneral

_etty

_elly

___ode Island

_uins

_entle

_ifle

_enuine

© Teacher Created Materials, Inc. 1986

IF YOU WERE IN A LOCKED ROOM WITH NOTHING BUT A BASEBALL BAT, HOW WOULD YOU GET OUT?

Sometimes words are not spelled exactly as they sound. You may have to look in more than one place in your dictionary before you find it. Below are two examples. For each word, choose the letter or letters which will complete it correctly. Circle the letter in that column as shown in the sample. Write the circled letters in the matching numbered blanks. Use your dictionary to check the spelling.

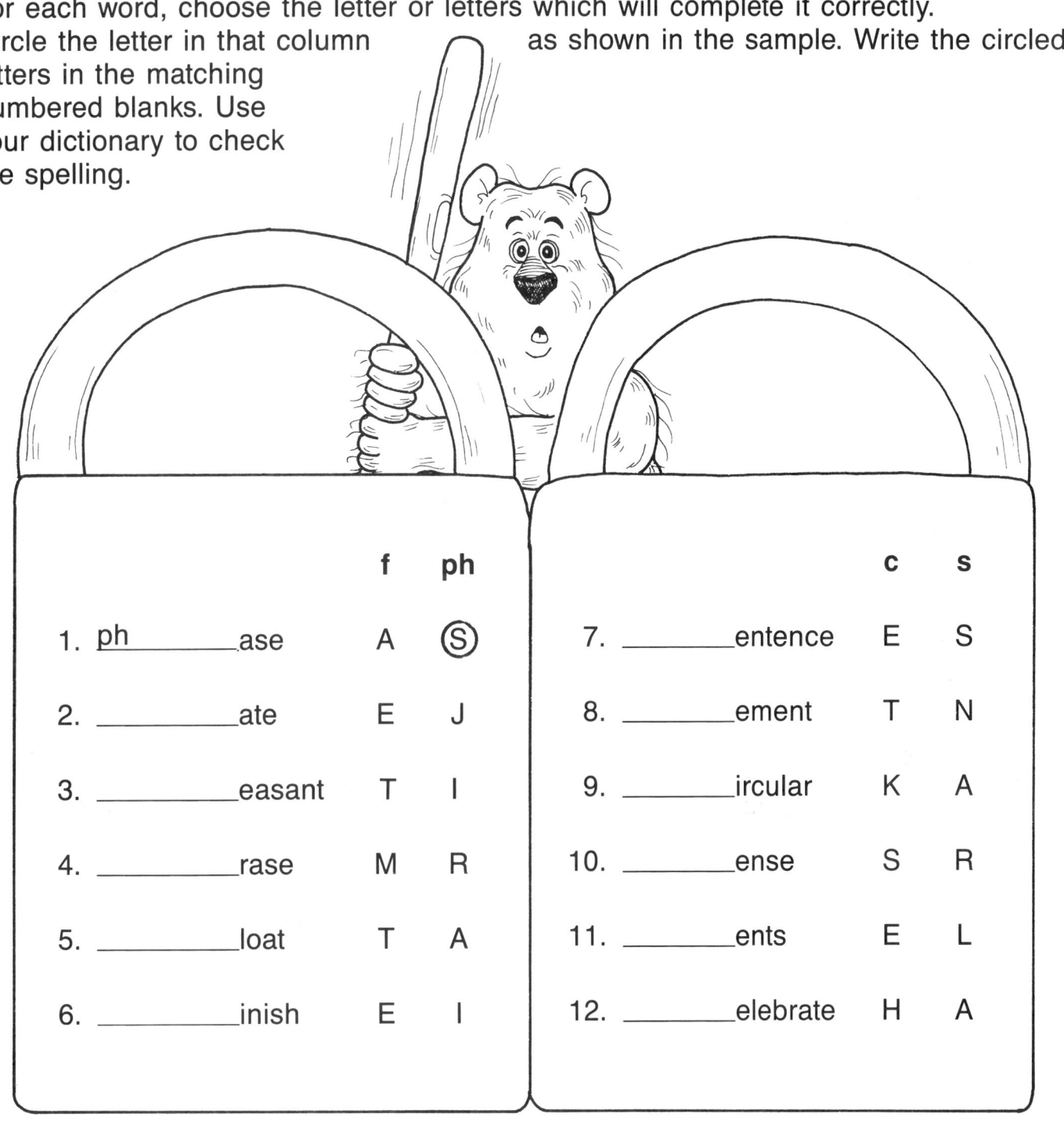

		f	ph				c	s
1. ph_____ase		A	Ⓢ		7. _____entence		E	S
2. _____ate		E	J		8. _____ement		T	N
3. _____easant		T	I		9. _____ircular		K	A
4. _____rase		M	R		10. _____ense		S	R
5. _____loat		T	A		11. _____ents		E	L
6. _____inish		E	I		12. _____elebrate		H	A

TAKE __ __ __ __ __   __ __ __ __ __ __ __ !
　　　 8　12　4　6　2　　 1　5　10　3　9　11　7

31

© Teacher Created Materials, Inc. 1986

ANNUAL MONSTER CONTEST

Enter your favorite monster in the yearly contest! It will win ten points for each correct answer you give below! Just fill in each blank with the correct letters. Use a dictionary if you need help.

KN or N

1. _____imble

2. _____uckle

3. _____eedle

4. _____it

5. _____eel

6. _____ightmare

R or WR

1. _____ong

2. _____ipen

3. _____eaper

4. _____estle

5. _____ench

6. _____ate

What is your monster's score? _____

Now draw your monster on the back of this sheet.

© Teacher Created Materials, Inc. 1986

SURPRISE PACKAGE

Dictionaries often give the plural endings of words. Write the plural spellings for these words. Then locate them in a dictionary to check yourself.

toga	campus	canoe	psaltery	kangaroo
osprey	mink	turkey	fantasy	discovery

Which of the above would you be most surprised to get for your birthday? On the back, name it and describe what you would do with it.

© Teacher Created Materials, Inc. 1986

THE LONG AND SHORT OF IT

You can find the meanings of abbreviations by looking in a dictionary. The way abbreviations are written may vary with different dictionaries. Locate each of these and write the most commonly used meaning.

1. I.O.U. _____

2. cm _____

3. Mr. _____

4. P.O. _____

5. no. _____

6. COD _____

7. mph _____

8. C _____

9. Ms. _____

10. lat. _____

11. D.S.T. _____

12. F _____

Write four more abbreviations and their meanings.

1. _____

2. _____

3. _____

4. _____

© Teacher Created Materials, Inc. 1986

ACRONYMS OUT OF THE HAT

An acronym is a word made from the first letters of a name. The set of letters is pronounced as a word. Locate these acronyms in a dictionary. Write the phonetic spellings and the meanings. For each word, name one person who would use it in daily matters.

> At least it's not me this time!
> I need a vacation.

UNICEF _____ _____

NOW _____ _____

AWOL _____ _____

WAF _____ _____

RADAR _____ _____

WAC _____ _____

NASA _____ _____

WAVES _____ _____

Now see if you can think of four more acronyms.
Write them on the back.

© Teacher Created Materials, Inc. 1986

TRACKING WORD ORIGINS

The words of the English language have many origins. These origins are shown after an entry in a dictionary. Look for the abbreviations to find out what language a word was taken from. Some words have been used in more than one language, having slightly different meanings in each.

For example: ballet FR fr. IT ballo, dance

Our word ballet came from French, and it came to French from Italian. Use a dictionary to locate the origins of these words. Draw the correct symbol beside each one.

△ Gk, Greek   🥦 It, Italian
⊗ F, French   ȣ L, Latin
✕ G, German

If possible, write the original word

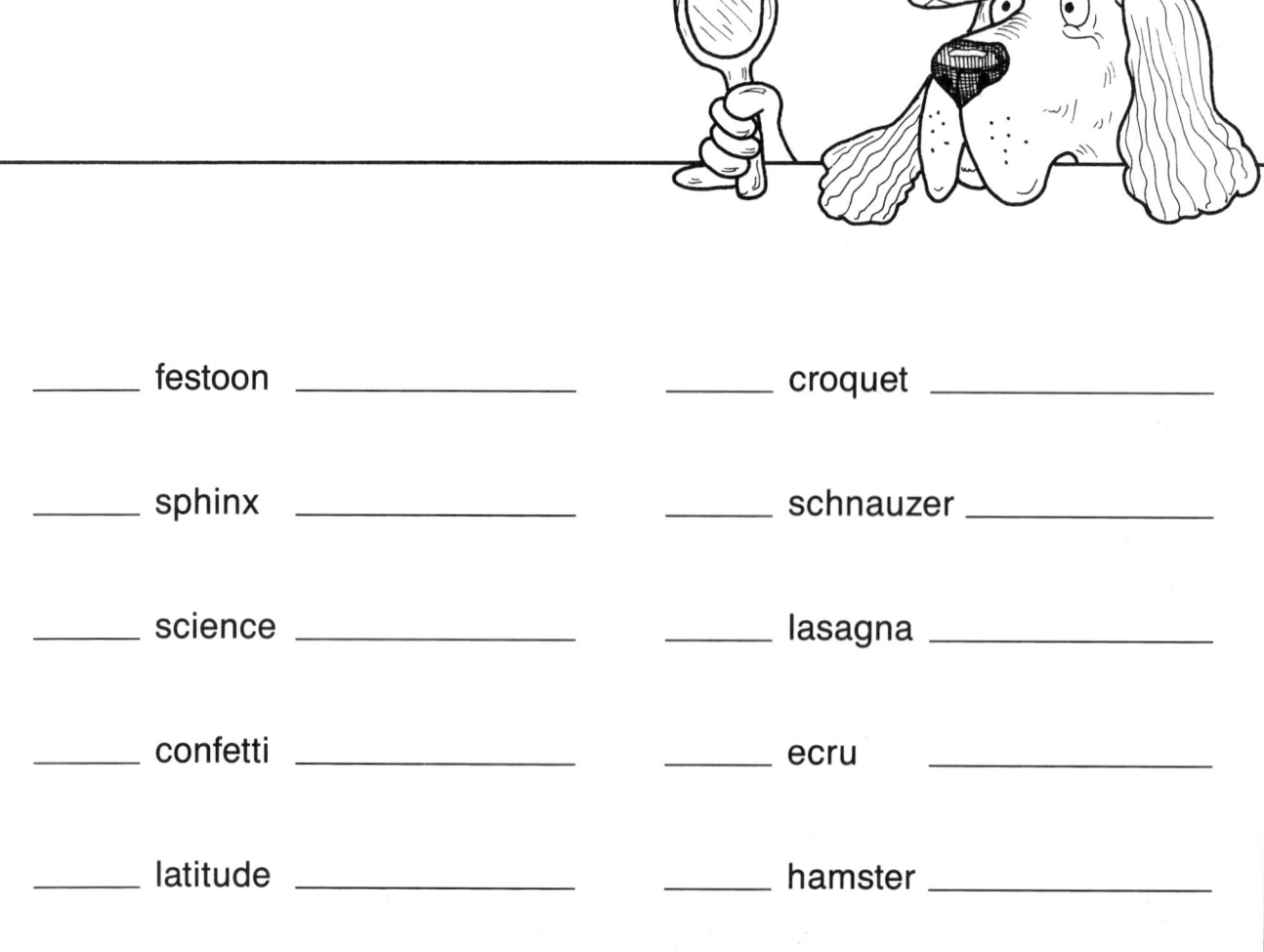

_____ festoon _____   _____ croquet _____

_____ sphinx _____   _____ schnauzer _____

_____ science _____   _____ lasagna _____

_____ confetti _____   _____ ecru _____

_____ latitude _____   _____ hamster _____

WANTED: DETECTIVE ASSISTANT

You can be Detective Doogle's research assistant! Here are your instructions: Locate each word in a dictionary. Write the language, or languages, it came from. Write the word's original meaning. Tell how the meaning we use is different from or like the original meaning.

parasol _____

_____

_____

kindergarten _____

_____

_____

malaria _____

_____

_____

goulash _____

_____

_____

quilt_____

_____

_____

peculiar _____

_____

_____

tent _____

_____

_____

On the back list four words of your own. Follow the directions above for each!

© Teacher Created Materials, Inc. 1986

BOWLED OVER!

Did you forget what a synonym is?
Look it up in your dictionary!

Look up each word in a dictionary. Then choose a synonym for each from below and write it. Mark through each word as you use it.

swell _____

vacant _____

injure _____

actual _____

petty _____

weighty _____

change _____

reduce _____

vision _____

reversed _____

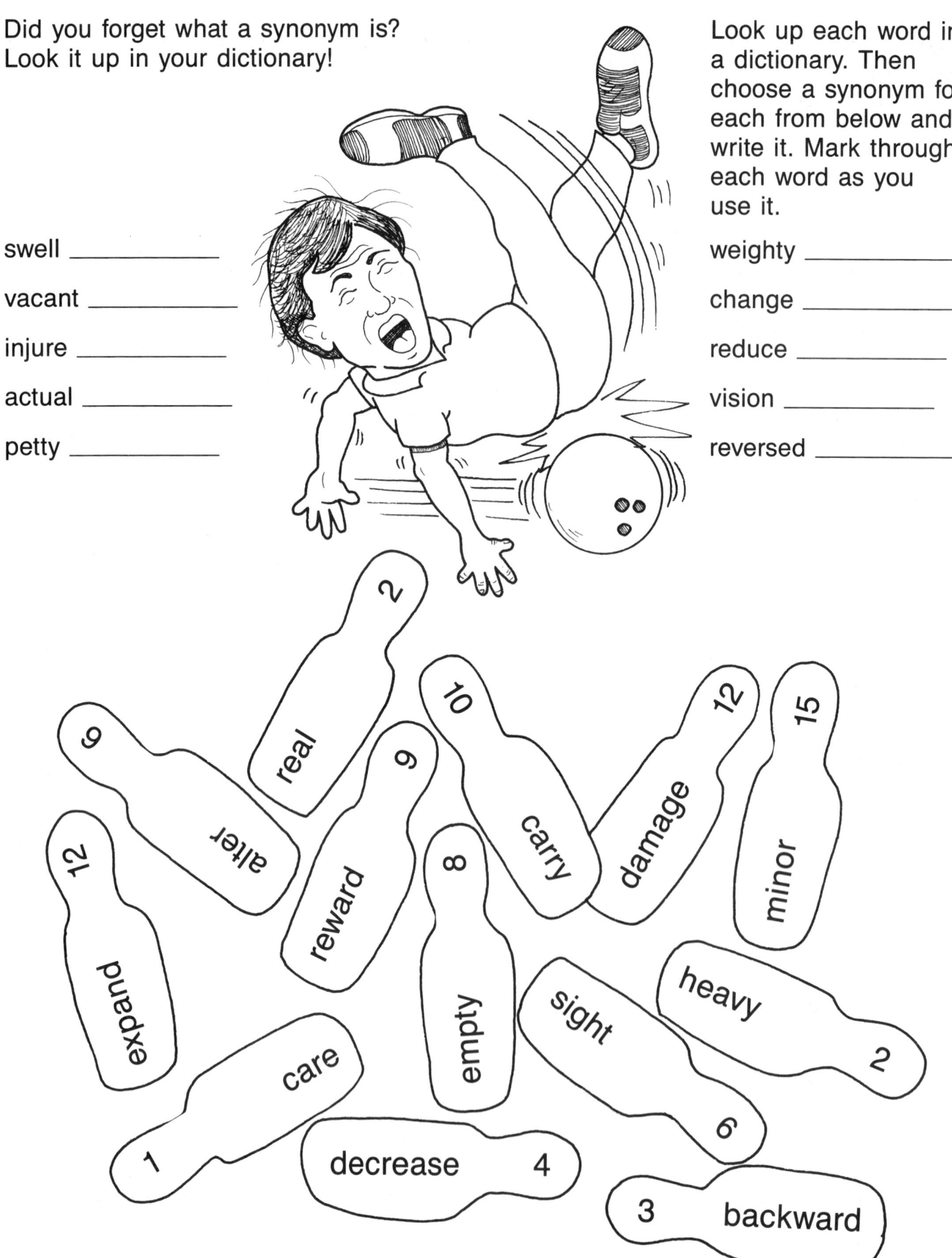

2

9

real

after

12

9

reward

10

carry

12

damage

15

minor

expand

8

empty

sight

heavy

care

decrease   4

6

1

3   backward

2

Now add the numbers from the pins you did not use. Is your total 20?

© Teacher Created Materials, Inc. 1986

WHAT A HOT SEAT!

Locate each of the numbered words in a dictionary. Read the definition. Choose an **antonym** from the smoke and write it on the line.
Did you forget what an antonym is? Look it up in your dictionary!

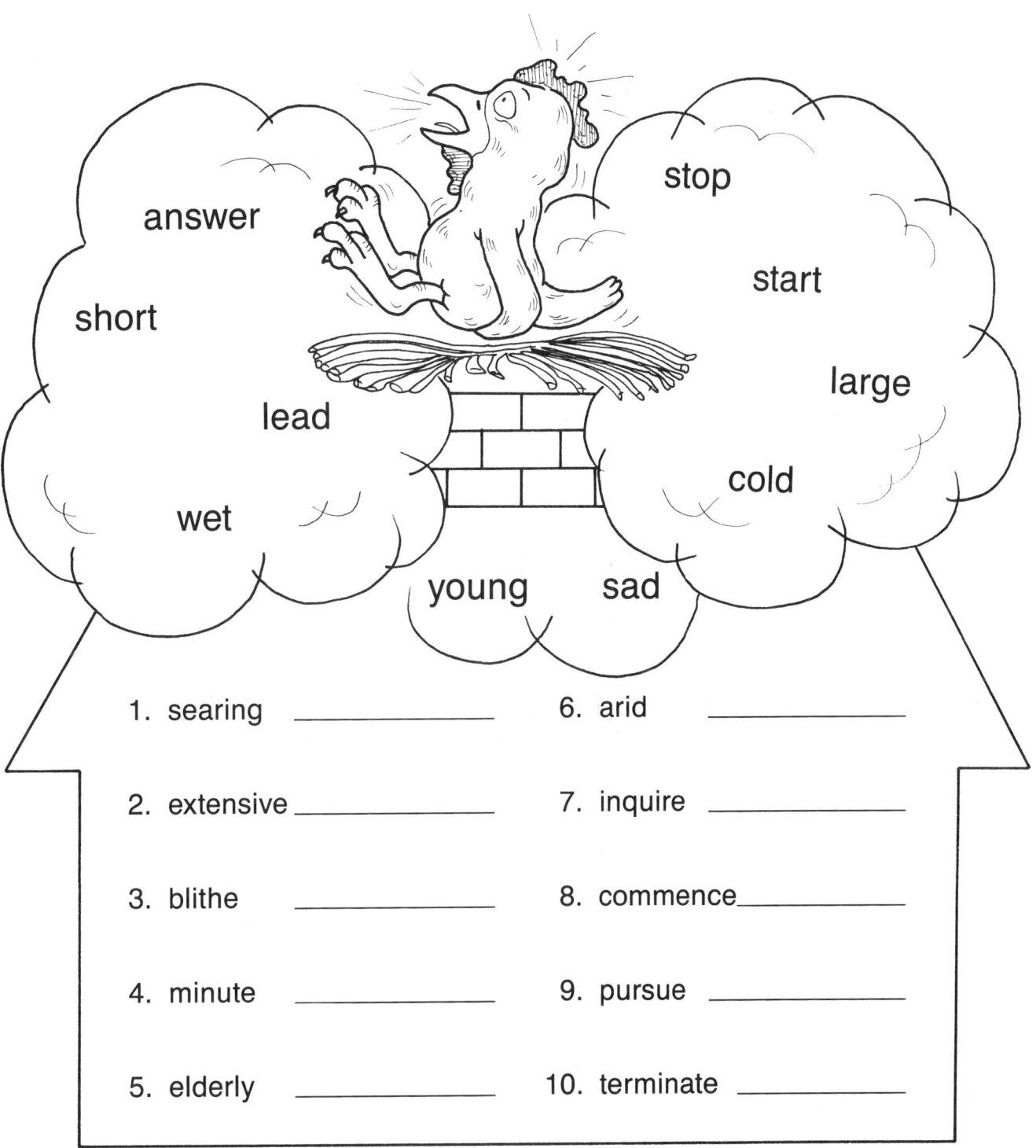

answer   stop   start   short   large   lead   cold   wet   young   sad

1. searing _____   6. arid _____

2. extensive _____   7. inquire _____

3. blithe _____   8. commence_____

4. minute _____   9. pursue _____

5. elderly _____   10. terminate _____

What will this poor bird do next? Write your answer on the back. Try to use at least four words from above.

    © Teacher Created Materials, Inc. 1986

WHAT FOLLOWED THE DINOSAURS?

Read each sentence. Match the definitions to the underlined words by writing the letters in the correct blanks. Use a dictionary if you need help. To answer the riddle, read down your column of letters.

_____ 1. Did the question <u>trip</u> you?

_____ 2. June likes to <u>trip</u> in the hall instead of walk.

_____ 3. Did you enjoy your <u>trip</u> to Hawaii?

_____ 4. I hope the rope doesn't <u>trip</u> anyone!

_____ 5. <u>Trip</u> the fire alarm if you smell smoke!

H. To move with a light step

R. To cause a mechanical action

I. To cause to fall

T. To cause someone to make a mistake

E. A journey

_____ 1. If the chimney won't <u>draw</u>, the fire won't burn.

_____ 2. We <u>draw</u> the curtains at night.

_____ 3. Cowboys must be able to <u>draw</u> their guns quickly.

_____ 4. Do you like to <u>draw</u> horses?

_____ 5. <u>Draw</u> the bedspread up neatly.

I. To pull from a holder

S. To move to a certain position

T. To cause a current of air to move

L. To use pencil or pen and make a picture

A. To close or shut

© Teacher Created Materials, Inc. 1986

SAFARI SNAPSHOTS

Many dictionaries include pictures to help you understand definitions. Locate each word to find out if it is a bird or beast, and what it looks like. List the words in alphabetical order under the correct heading. Draw a picture of each animal.

| oryx | auk | ptmarmigan | pangolin |
| emu | lemur | margay | hornbill |

BIRDS

BEASTS

Be sure you can pronounce each name!

41

PACKING ROOM PUZZLER

Shari has a real problem! She must pack these items in four different cartons, but she doesn't know what they are! Locate each in a dictionary. Code each item for Shari by drawing the correct symbol in the box.

△ something to eat
♥ something to wear
8 something to ride
O something to do

1. ☐ yacht

2. ☐ croquet

3. ☐ ascot

4. ☐ endives

5. ☐ chapeau

6. ☐ obi

7. ☐ strudel

8. ☐ ricksha

9. ☐ quoits

10. ☐ pantaloons

11. ☐ lacrosse

12. ☐ sulky

13. ☐ rutabaga

14. ☐ tunic

15. ☐ succotash

© Teacher Created Materials, Inc. 1986

LET'S SEE SOME ACTION!

Look up each of these words in a dictionary and read the definitions. Use them to answer the questions.

shove	vault	yank	scale	amble
dash	fling	trill	bellow	snatch

1. How do you reach the top of a mountain? _____

2. Do you trill or bellow if your house is on fire? _____

3. How do you get across a mud puddle? _____

4. If you amble to school, do you get there quickly? _____

5. How do you win a foot race? _____

6. How do you get rid of a frisbee? _____

7. What happens if you yank a tooth? _____

8. If your car won't start, how do you move it? _____

9. Would you snatch a hot plate? _____

Choose one word and draw a picture on the back to show what it means.

© Teacher Created Materials, Inc. 1986

DESCRIBE IT TO ME

Locate the words below in a dictionary and read the definitions. Use them to complete the puzzle.

ACROSS

1. The _____ hair scratched my face.

2. The _____ spider didn't hurt her.

4. An _____ person might not finish his work.

5. A _____ flash hurt my eyes.

9. The _____ man had not eaten for weeks.

10. The _____ child didn't like to meet strangers.

DOWN

3. The piano was too wide to fit through the _____ door.

6. He could not answer the _____ questions.

7. Her _____ skin was as white as a sheet.

8. The _____ water barely moved.

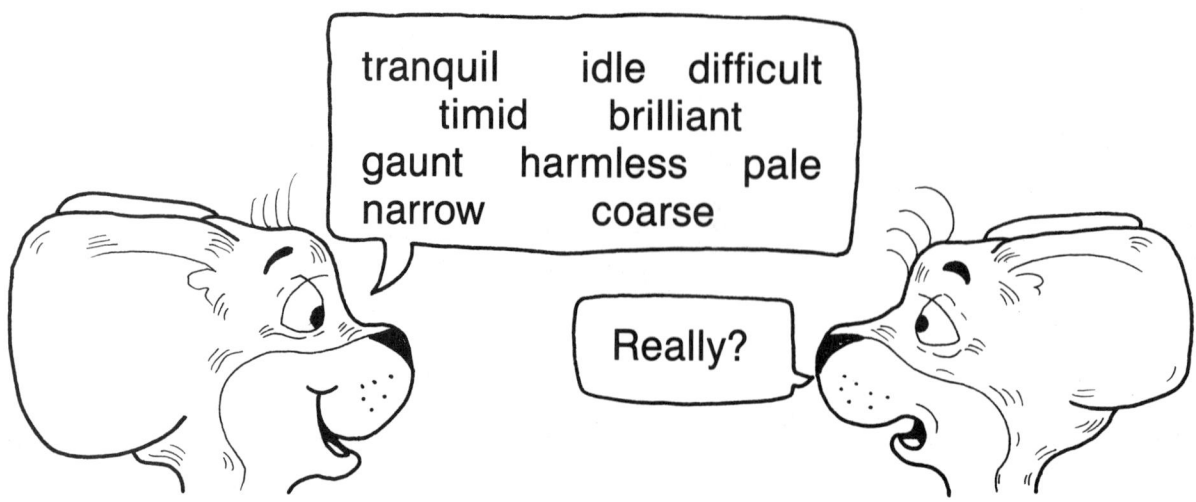

tranquil   idle   difficult
   timid   brilliant
gaunt   harmless   pale
narrow   coarse

Really?

WHAT BEAUTIFUL COLORS!

Look up each of these words in a dictionary and read the definition.
Answer the questions.

indigo   olive   cinnamon

lilac   ecru   cerulean

scarlet   ochre   khaki

magenta

1. If barns are usually painted red, could they
   ever be painted scarlet? _____
2. Which could be ochre: a lime or a banana? _____
3. Could an indigo bunting hide in the grass?_____
4. Would lilac be a better color for a king's robe or
   a business suit? _____
5. If you spilled ecru paint on white paper, would it show up very well? _____
   Why?_____
6. What color would a cinnamon bear be? _____
7. If you were painting the sky and the sea, which should be cerulean? ____
8. Is khaki a good color for clothes you might get very dirty? _____
   Why?_____
9. If you were looking for olive and magenta Easter eggs in tall grass, which
   would be easier to see? _____

Now color the spots as closely as you can to the colors given.

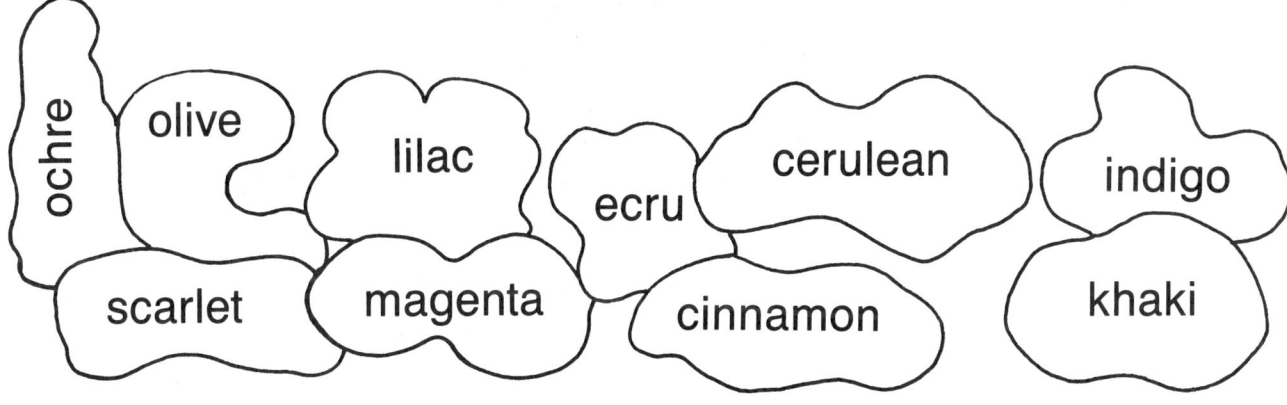

© Teacher Created Materials, Inc. 1986

TOOLS OF THE TRADE

Look up these words in a dictionary and read the definitions. Answer the questions.

whisk	thesaurus	palette	trowel	gaff
easel	colander	planetarium	silo	chisel

1. Would you find an apple tree in a **planetarium**? _____

2. What is the difference between a **trowel** and a **chisel**? _____
   _____

3. What would you see if you looked in a **thesaurus**? _____
   _____

4. Would you want to taste something on a **palette**? _____

5. If you were looking at a **whisk**, would you be in a barber's
   shop? _____

6. Would you rather pick up a **colander** or a **silo**? _____

7. Is it easy to move an **easel**? _____

8. Would you use a **gaff** on land or at sea? _____

Write the tools from above beside the workers who would use them.

cook _____   sculptor _____

fisherman _____   artist _____

astronomer_____   farmer _____

writer_____   gardener _____

ANSWER PAGE

Page 4: **ACROSS:** 1) Illustrations, 3) Acronym, 4) Meanings, 6) Synonyms, 8)Pronunciation
DOWN: 2) Abbreviations, 5) Etymology, 7) Capital, 9) Antonyms, 10) Syllables

Page 5:

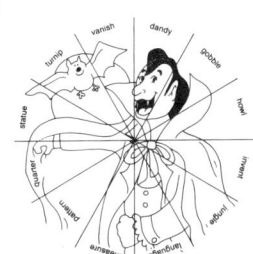

Page 24:

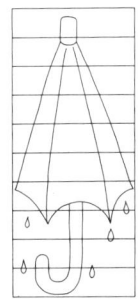

Page 25:

Page 6: **ABCD** - aunt, begin, canvas, creek, desert, **EFGHIJKL** - exit, garage, huge, jam, landing, **MNOPQR** - money, open, pair, pet, ready, **STUVWXYZ** - stray, underneath, vacant, wood, zebra

Page 7: 1) Canary, 2) Crow, 3) Eagle, 4) Egret, 5) Finch, 6) Flamingo, 7) Kingfisher, 8) Osprey, 9) Ostrich, 10) Peacock, 11) Pigeon, 12) Seagull, 13) Starling
Answer to the riddle: THE BIG CHICKEN!

Page 8: Answers will vary.

Page 9: 1) I, 2) P, 3) B, 4) L, 5) O, 6) I, 7) T, 8) U, 9) G, 10) H, 11) L, 12) N, 13) A, 14) N, 15) N, 16) Y
Answer to the riddle: BY BONING UP ALL NIGHT!

Page 10: 1) E, 2) T, 3) N, 4) T, 5) T, 6) I, 7) A, 8) N, 9) Y, 10) K, 11) C, 12) H
Answer to riddle: BECAUSE THEY CAN'T KNIT!

Page 11: **CALL/CAP** - calves, camel, candle, canopy, **CHEAP/CHEMICAL** - cheat, check, cheetah, chef, **COLD/COMMENT** - colony, color, combine, comic, **COW/CREAM** - cowboy, coy, crab, cracker

Page 12: Answers will vary depending on dictionary used

Page 13: Answers will vary depending on dictionary used

Page 14: Answers will vary depending on dictionary used

Page 15: boiling point, candle power, pocket book, canary yellow, flying saucer, potato chip, river bed
Answers may vary with different dictionaries.

Page 16: 1) D, 2) I, 3) C, 4) T, 5) I, 6) O, 7) N, 8) A, 9) R, 10) Y = DICTIONARY

Page 17: Help, I'm stranded on an island. Please send a boat quickly. I don't want to leave. I just need a television and a very long electrical cord.

Page 18: tickle, famous, city, canvas, goldfish, after, ponies, icy, bases, reply, funny, runway
Answer to riddle: BY LONG DISTANCE!

Page 19: **One-syllable words:** rough, route, steal, timed, halt, **Two-syllable words:** quiet, muscle, timid, bargain, **Three-syllable words:** impatient, umbrella, furniture, **Four-syllable words:** necessary, kindergarten

Page 20: to ma'to, pump'kins, ba nan'a, pep'pers, cab'bage, tur'nips, blue'berr"y, sau'sage, lem on ade', po ta'toes, wa'ter mel"on, oat'meal

Page 21: 1) eye-lash, 2) slen-der, 3) peace-ful, 4) chim-pan-zee, 5) wil-low, 6) bath-tub, 7) sad-dle, 8) yes-ter-day, 9) chick-en, 10) o-pos-sum, 11) um-brel-la, 12) bal-loons

Page 22: **Yellow Words:** beneath, china, final, tiger, seaport, protect, human
Blue Words: balance, canoe, lemon, salute, vanish, magic, sugar, travel, level

Page 23: **Suffixes -** 1) ful, 2) ment, 3) ly, 4) al, 5) ive, 6) ist, 7) ness, 8) ic, 9) ly, 10) ness
Individual answers for definitions will vary.

Page 24: 1) simplify, 2) baker, 3) beautiful, 4) washable, 5) penniless, 6) bakery, 7) skillful, 8) teacher, 9) childhood, 10) wooden
Drawing is on top of this page.

Page 25: 1) unclear, 2) prepay, 3) presoak, 4) misunderstand, 5) rewrite, 6) bimonthly, 7) overpay, 8) antiwar, 9) midnight, 10) rearrange. Drawing is on top of this page.

© *Teacher Created Materials, Inc. 1986*

ANSWER PAGE

Page 26: autobus, autobiography, autoharp, biweekly, bicycle, disobey, reglue, retire, repack, recycle, dislocate, relocate, unpack, unglue, untie

Page 27: 1) appear, 2) trust, 3) person, 4) courage, 5) think, 6) pay, 7) correct, 8) arrange, 9) act, 10) attach, 11) joy

Page 28: 1) D, 2) T, 3) H, 4) N, 5) H, 6) R, 7) T, 8) W, 9) O, 10) U, 11) O, 12) S, 13) E, 14) T, 15) O
Answer to the riddle: THE DOOR WON'T SHUT!

Page 29: 1) verb, 2) adjective, 3) noun, 4) verb, 5) adverb, 6) adjective, 7) noun, 8) adverb, 9) adjective, 10) noun
Sentences will vary.

Page 30: **R-Words:** road, rifle, ruins, **RH-Words:** rhubarb, rhyme, Rhode Island, **G-Words:** general, gentle, genuine, gelatin, **J-Words:** jelly, jetty, jealous

Page 31: 1) S, 2) E, 3) I, 4) R, 5) T, 6) E, 7) S, 8) T, 9) K, 10) R, 11) E, 12) H
Answer to the riddle: TAKE THREE STRIKES!

Page 32: 1) n, 2) kn, 3) n, 4) kn, 5) kn, 6) n
1) wr, 2) r, 3) r, 4) wr, 5) wr, 6) r

Page 33: **toga** - togas or togae, **campus** - campuses, **kangaroo** - kangaroos or kangaroo, **psaltery** - psalteries, **canoe** - canoes, **discovery** - discoveries, **mink** - minks or mink, **turkey** - turkeys or turkey, **fantasy** - fantasies, **osprey** - ospreys

Page 34: 1) I owe you, 2) centimeter, 3) Mister, 4) Post Office, 5) number, 6) cash/collect on delivery, 7) miles per hour, 8) centigrade, celcius, 9) Miss or Mrs., 10) latitude, 11) Daylight Saving Time, 12) Fahrenheit

Page 35: **UNICEF:** United Nations International Children's Emergency Fund, **NOW:** National Organization of Women, **AWOL:** Absent Without Leave, **WAF:** Women in the Air Force, **RADAR**, radio detecting and ranging, **WAC:** Women's Army Corps, **NASA:** National Aeronautics and Space Administration, **WAVES**, Women Accepted for Volunteer Emergency Service

Page 36: Answers may vary.

Page 37: Answers will vary.

Page 38: swell-expand, vacant-empty, injure-damage, actual-real, petty-minor, weighty-heavy, change-alter, reduce-decrease, vision-sight, reversed-backward

Page 39: 1) cold, 2) short, 3) sad, 4) large, 5) young, 6) wet, 7) answer, 8) stop, 9) lead, 10) start

Page 40: 1) T, 2) H, 3) E, 4) I, 5) R
1) T, 2) A, 3) I, 4) L, 5) S

Page 41: **Birds:** Auk, Emu, Ptmarigan, Hornbill. **Beasts:** Oryx, Pangolin, Lemur, Margay.

Page 42: 1) 8, 2) O, 3) ❤, 4) △, 5) ❤, 6) ❤, 7) △, 8) 8, 9) O, 10) ❤, 11) O, 12) 8, 13) △, 14) ❤, 15) △

Page 43: 1) scale, 2) bellow, 3) vault, 4) no, 5) dash, 6) fling, 7) (pull it), 8) shove, 9) no

Page 44: **ACROSS:** 1) coarse, 2) harmless, 4) idle, 5) brilliant, 9) gaunt, 10) timid
DOWN: 3) narrow, 6) difficult, 7) pale, 8) tranquil

Page 45: 1) Yes, 2) Banana, 3) No, 4) King's robe, 5) No. Because it is a very light tan color, 6) Reddish-brown, 7) Sky, 8) Yes, the dirt won't show up on the clothes, 9) Magenta

Page 46: 1) No, 2) trowel-digging, chisel-breaks stone, 3) words, 4) No, 5) No, 6) colander, 7) Yes, 8) sea
cook - whisk, colander; **fisherman** - gaff; **astronomer** - planetarium; **writer** - thesaurus; **sculptor** - chisel; **artist** - easel, palette; **farmer** - silo; **gardener** - trowel